Other titles
by
Corey Hamilton

Keep Left
Society's Grip
Exit Is A Safe Place
No One
Shall Be Spared Open Up
Mash Notes
Mash Notes: vol 2
Too Personal
2 Days Unhyped
Time Marches On
Thirty Three
VI
What If?
Magic Bus
How I Remember It
Cease & Desist
Sensible Shoes
Do Not Ever Have Any Good Ideas
DNA
I Am NOT With The Band
Wedge Politics
My Side Project

Lonely Night Songs

Copyright © 2008 Corey Hamilton

All rights reserved. No part of this book may be reproduced or transmitted in any form or by any means, graphic, mechanical or electronic, including photocopying and recording, or by any information storage or retrieval system without written permission from the publisher, except for brief passages quoted in review.

Library and Archives Canada Cataloguing in Publication

Hamilton, Corey, 1971-
Lonely night songs / Corey Hamilton.

Poems.
ISBN 978-1-926623-00-9

    I. Title.

PS8565.A5347L66 2009   C811'.54   C2008-906587-5

All writing and photography by Corey Hamilton © 2008.

Book layout and design by Corey Hamilton.

First Printing

Published by Dramatic Situations
       P.O. Box 696
       Edmonton, AB
       T5J 2L4
       CANADA
www.dramaticsituations.com

Lonely Night Songs

A book of poetry, prose & photography

by

Corey Hamilton

"Just Plain Tired"

"Introduce Yourself"

It started in the late spring. I am not sure when it ended but it must have, because it tore a part out of me.

"Tired Sisters"

We ran into each other twice, and when I said that you would get sick of me, I was actually placating you. For what I really meant was, I would get sick of you.

While I was thinking about all of that, you said the same thing to me, that I just said to you. You probably even thought the same thing as me too. So we placated each other. After the circle jerk, you talked about your mother's bad relationship with her current boyfriend and how, "men always get their way in a divorce."

It sounds like you do too much dope and alcohol. Oh, you do do too much dope and alcohol. It has never been so obvious as that conversation.

The people who call me sometimes don't know english very well. I should get paid extra for being a translator.

All of a sudden things were going good. She said that I was "a real person", and even gave me a hug. Then I made a mistake and she never talked to me again.

I guess "a real person" doesn't make mistakes. I was told that if humans never forgot anything that they would go insane. I guess I can forget you and then I would be safe from going insane.

My Dad's mother is dying right now and all I can think about is my next paycheck.

It took me 24 hours to forget about my paycheck. With a bit of a struggle, I did forget it and moved on. Now I am even more safe from going insane.

The girl with the dyed orange hair who smokes ultra-slims, and is just way too cool to smile, is wearing 1950 era white rimmed sunglasses. They are big and round just like her breasts.

I saw the girl with the dyed orange hair again. This time she was wearing a skin tight shirt which showed off her breasts. Her bare arms were slick with rain water and she looked beautiful, but the bible she was reading and her cigarettes turned me off.

Years ago, my Grandmother Hamilton was getting out of the van with my Grandfather and she slammed one of her fingers in the door. My Grandfather was so proud of her for not crying even though she nearly took off one finger and bled all over the place. She never cried.

When I told my Grandmother this, she said to me that "there was no need to cry." The tone that she said it with made it seem like the thought of her crying for nearly losing a finger just did NOT make sense to her.

When Grandpa Hamilton would start a food fight, Grandma would say, "Oh Ronald."

I was never sure if she was ticked off at Grandpa for making such a mess (which made more work for her) or if she was touched by how much he cared about their Grandchildren. If it was the latter, she just may not have minded the mess because she in turn loved her Grandchildren very much too.

So she probably was a little annoyed but put up with the mess because it was Grandpa and us Grandchildren doing it.

If the heaven that you believed in exists, and you are now there and if you are lifting hay bails or watching, "Dancing With The Stars," I sincerely hope that you are at peace with yourself. Knowing that you were the best wife, Mother, Grandmother, Great-Grandmother, sister, Aunt and our best friend.

It is raining everywhere and even though I am not a religious or spiritual person, something in me hopes that Grandma H. and Grandpa H. are together now.

My youngest cousin on the Hamilton side tried on my Grandmother's wedding dress from 1942. Even though it was falling apart, it fit perfectly and she looked beautiful.

I saw her twice yesterday.

The first time she did not notice me.

She was a skater girl with a long board to ride on. She had a purple mohawk with blonde on the sides of her head. When she got on the same bus as me I noticed that she was chubby but had a nice bounce.

She sat down close to me and I smiled at her. It looked like my smile surprised her because she did not smile back. She looked tired.

Grandma Hamilton's 4 sisters that could make it to the funeral looked sad and tired. One of their husbands (the only other one alive could not make it) looked the same.

Hope and anticipation.

Lip gloss, rock star sunglasses, long brown hair and big brown eyes keeping it quiet in the bar, once and for all. All of the pretty girls that I work with get tired of me talking to them or even me looking at them.

The Chinese girl with the speech impediment said that all black people look the same. I felt like saying, "black people probably think that all of you Asians look the same." Fuckwad.

The girl to my right has blonde hair and lots of piercings. Very pretty, but she is pretty typical too. I.E.: she knows that she is pretty and she is just too cool to smile.

She lights a smoke and juggles her bus fair in her hand with the wedding band on it and leans back.

My Grandma Hamilton never failed anyone, even in her passing away, I know now that it is better this way because she was suffering and anyone with a heart that big should not have to suffer.

My Father, his 3 younger brothers and his younger sister all looked tired at the funeral. They have moved on just great and I am very proud of them all. They all have my respect.

She had the most patience of anyone in the family. I learned a lot from her. With all of my problems and my pains in the neck, I know that (even in death) she came through for me and was never judgmental.

How do you become a "pop culture expert?"

Is there a two year course at a technical school for that? I wonder if you call yourself a "pop culture expert," then do you work at a "Subway" restaurant to support your avid buying of all that crap? Are you a "sandwich artist" too? I mean that is pretty much the same as saying you are a "pop culture expert," just less media coverage.

Am I out of line?

Waiting for the bus and some young Asian girl is sitting to my left talking rapidly on her cell-phone about how much she partied last night. She is pretty and her english is perfect. She finishes the call and quickly calls someone else. Cell-phones and people who can't stop talking on them make me want to take a shit in their laps. Thankfully, her bus came and she left.

She is always sick and doesn't know what she is doing. I HATE working with her as a supervisor.

Are you gettin' lippy with me, boy?

It is much easier to be an asshole than a nice guy. The lady who cursed me out in the winter because I had devil horns on my toque, thanked me today because I opened the door for her at the post office that I always see her at. I guess that she did not recognize me without my "horns." I bit my tongue and helped her out.

I went out for lunch today and noticed four young people. Three pretty Asian girls and one pretty black boy. One by one they finished their food and went to the washroom.
Pretty black boy.
1) Gorgeous Asian girl with nice legs.
2) Gorgeous Asian girl with big breasts.
3) Cute Asian girl with a white top on.

They all got back to the table and paid for their food. Asian girl #1 put money in the pretty black boy's front pocket of his jeans. Then they all went outside and Asian girl #2 wiped something off of the pretty black boy's face. Asian girl #3 looked uncomfortable. Asian girls #1 and #2 looked at the pretty black boy hungrily even though they had just ate. The four of them walked away.

I propositioned the owner of the restaurant I am in and she laughed and smiled a wonderful smile. Just then the pretty black boy and the three Asian girls strolled by the window. Asian girl #2 was holding the pretty black boy's hand.

Maybe Asian girl #3 is tired. Maybe the owner of this restaurant is tired of being propositioned by poor, fat men.

I think about you every day and how you struggled the last few years of your life. Especially struggling in the last 2 weeks of your life. Rest in peace Grandma H., rest in peace.

The cute Asian girl I smiled at returned the smile with a smile but still would not sit next to me.

She comes off as if she doesn't know what she is doing with her nervous laughter, stuttering and running around like a chicken with its head cut off.

The other day I was walking behind you. We were both crossing the same street and it was very windy. You had long brown hair and you were wearing a long brown dress that suddenly blew up and showed your perfect legs and the white underwear you had on.

Casually, you pulled your dress down as if this sort of thing happens to you all of the time, and you kept on walking. You seemed tired. I will never see you again, even though I know that one is not supposed to say "never."

A small quirky song floats through my head while I ride the bus towards my destination.

I am the only male on the bus. The rest of the people are all young or old women all of them wearing perfumes that waft into my nose. All these smells will probably not be easily forgotten. I saw her again.

This is the second time in one week. the last time I saw her, before the first time this week, was almost 20 years ago. We were on a bus and I was whacked out on mushrooms. She still has lots of energy and she doesn't seem tired. Quite a refreshing change from most of the women I meet from that time period in my life. Usually they have changed into tired sisters.

A pleasant surprise indeed.

The lady who cleans up where I work doesn't know english very well, so I try to make her smile and chit chat with her.

One day the lady looked really sad. I asked what was wrong and in her broken english she said that her back was extremely sore. Soon her boss who knew english perfectly was there vacuuming. The boss did NOT look happy. I felt like telling her to suck it up. The boss hadn't looked like she had done that sort of work or even gotten her hands dirty in years. Dumb ass.

In all of the noise and commotion of the busy cafe where I waited for a friend, outside was a co-worker with her Grandson. The co-worker and I waved at each other and I made her Grandson smile by making faces at him.

They were a nice contrast to the noise in the cafe.

When my co-worker saw that I made her Grandson smile, she smiled too. What a wonderful way to start the day.

I am a beautiful woman. I know it. I should be a super model. Do you see how I hold my cigarette? I am beautiful but don't look at me.

*Author's Note: She is a **FAKE** tired sister.*

Hair stylists are some of the most brainless and self absorbed people around. They honestly think that they are so important and they get snotty if you give them their attitude right back.

I took an order from one the other day. She started off by saying that her and her co-workers order from us all of the time. I checked. They had ordered 3 times before today. I barely got through the order without hunting her down at her local address and beating her senseless. So I asked her how she wanted to pay for her order; cash, credit or debit. She replied, "Mastercard." I repeat- ed back the total and Mastercard and she yelled, "I said Visa!!!" So I repeated back the total and Visa and she yelled again, "I meant Mastercard!!!" She hung up before I could tell her how long before she could expect her order.

MORON.

You cut hair, you don't operate on brains, YOU FUCKING MORON.

I am a beautiful woman. I know it. I should be a super model. Do you see how I hold my cigarette? I am beautiful but don't look at me unless you are beautiful by my shallow standards. I should get a baby t-shirt that says, "I am beautiful, but don't look at me unless you are beautiful."

*Author's Note: If I saw a shallow sister wearing that shirt I would stick a sign on her back that said, "I am a **FAKE** tired sister," instead of, "Kick me."*

*Correction: I would put two signs on her back. The first, "I am a **FAKE** tired sister," and the second, "Kick me."*

I was walking downtown and I had just stopped at a red light when I noticed a young Asian girl standing to my left. She had beautiful long hair, big beautiful brown eyes and a nice face. The light turned green and we started walking. I suddenly noticed her legs, actually her calves. They were monstrous, just huge! Her thighs and ass were both big and solid. Her upper body was covered by a white sweater but one could tell that she was a body builder.

You know the type; the men, no penis and no hair (except on their head) and all of those huge muscles. Steroid monkeys are what I call them.

As for the women, no penis and no hair (except on their head), no breasts and all of those huge muscles. Some of the women (like in wrestling) have the big fake boobs. This woman was not small in the chest department, but she was not big either. In other words, no big fake boobs.

I looked at her pretty face again and she caught me and then glared at me. But before I could ask her if she does steroids she did a b-line (no shit, coincidence or not?) for the gym. I looked at my extra 60 pounds and felt uncomfortable. I then caught the next bus home a little sad.

What about the young, elitist girl with the transvestite father? The young, elitist girl with the transvestite father won't listen to Reggae because she "isn't black," yet she listens to hip hop?

Fake tired sister! Fake!

I was on the bus going from the University to downtown and these two young pretty girls got on the bus and sat at the front and talked about Whyte Avenue. One of the girls had long brown hair, big blue eyes and is well tanned. The other girl had short red hair and is whiter than me. The girl with the long brown hair said, "I called my Mom and asked if we could get picked up by her if there was any sort of a problem, like getting beat up."

I felt like saying to them that if this was their first time to "The Ave" and it is just before 10 in the morning on a saturday, then you are relatively safe. I kept my yap shut and watched them get off in the middle of it all and I kept on heading towards downtown.

I hoped that nothing happens to them to turn them into tired sisters.

She told me to tuck in my shirt because it did not look good. I thought to myself, I am a fucking pallbearer at someone's funeral. That someone was my Grandmother Hamilton. The "girl" who told me this was one of my sisters. She was giving me shit again. I thought of telling her off and then thought better of it because some things are futile. Like getting my family to lay off of me. I still did not tuck in my shirt. I was tired then and I am still tired to this very day.

A young girl with dyed red hair (not cartoon red, yet dyed nonetheless) and fishnets on her forearms is listening to her MP3 player, holding a bag and holding her transfer. She looks as tired of life as I am right now. I am tired of everything collapsing on and around me. I am tired of things never working out.

She looks the same way that I feel. I get on my bus and go home, watching her as the bus leaves with me on it. I leave behind another lame day. Third in a row actually.

One of the new East Indian ladies at the 7-11 asked me a few questions the last time I saw her there. They were as follows: Do you like women? Do you have kids? Are you married?

I told her yes about the first and no to the second two questions. The last 2 questions I said that maybe they will happen. And that I am patient. Then I left and went home wondering why she asked me those questions and if the latter two will indeed come true. I guess only time will tell. Overall the conversation was kind of creepy, especially when you consider that the woman is married with at least 1 child. Very creepy indeed.

I am taking care of one of the plants of this other lady. She seems like a nice woman although she has cancelled meeting with me twice, including this morning. I don't want to get my hopes up. I will see what happens when she gets home, like if she makes time for me.

This tall fat chick with bleach blonde hair I used to know has given me the cold shoulder the last three times I have run into her. She's the one who always latched onto Seattle bands in the early 90's when it was cool to do so. She is a real phony pisshead.

What goes around, comes around fat cow.

Except for a few, most teenage girls are fucking insane. They cry at the drop of a hat or flip out and get angry at the drop of a hat.

I have proof of this:
1) I grew up with two younger sisters.
2) I went to school with my fair share of girls.
3) When I was 23 I was seeing an 18 year old girl. She was fucking nuts. Crying in public, getting angry at me for being an Atheist and finally she was going out with another guy at the same time she was going out with me. When I confronted her about the other guy she basically told me to piss off. Then when I got emotional she got angry with me. Hello pot! Here's the kettle calling!

Again, what goes around, comes around bitchcakes.
She told me things that could have got her arrested.
She left me. I guess when you gotta go, you gotta go.

Since your show last month I have often wondered what I would have said to you had we met. Or better yet, what you would have said, if anything. Your voice and music got me through some tough times and they still do get me through some tough times.

I guess I could have started by saying, "Thank you."
Waiting 3 hours. In the middle they take my blood and I wait again.
The nurses here are fantastic! Seriously. They put up with all of the abuse when I am sure that they are tired. One male nurse and the rest are sisters. When I leave, I will tell them what a great job they all do. Thanks gals and guy, thanks.

They checked me again and I told them what a great job they do. I hope that they believed me. More waiting....

I was waiting in my Doctor's office and an over-weight woman in a suit came in saying that she had an appointment today. When the woman behind the counter said that there was no appointment for her today, that fat suit woman got angry and raised her voice still saying, "I have an appointment today! I confirmed it 3 times! Yes, you have an appointment on the 6th for me!"

The woman behind the counter calmly stated, "Today is the 5th."

Bitch suit woman then said,"Oh...is there anything open today?"

When the woman behind the counter said no, the bitch stormed out. The woman behind the counter didn't even get an apology from the bitch. I should have followed the bitch out and curbed her for being so ignorant and disrespectful.

I told the three women behind the counter that they should not listen to her because they are doing a great job. The three of them behind the counter should get medals for putting up with all of the shit that they put up with.

There were so many questions I would have liked to ask her when I saw her this morning.... Is she a single mother?

Does she have a husband or boyfriend or lover?

Is the father of her child dead or just dead in her heart?

Is she bitter about men in general?

Would she like to take another chance, this time, with a guy like me? Etcetera, etcetera, etcetera....

There is so much I would like to tell her about me. Maybe it will come later, maybe, maybe....

The cute young girl at the restaurant I go to often treats me really nice. It is really great to go there. She may be a lesbian. She sort of has that look. Or she may be taken. Regardless, she is awesome to deal with. I may ask her out and see what happens. That restaurant has a good track record of hiring nice staff. Being a waitress or a waiter is a tough job. Even if the females who work there won't go out with me, they still have my respect.

The young girl inputs into her cell-phone the date and time of my next poetry reading, while I hum a song by "Slayer" to myself. What are we going to do with all of the women who can't make up their minds? I love women who know exactly what they want.

I am tired of you and your fakeness. At your funeral they will read, "The Catcher In The

Rye." At my funeral there will be a war dance.

Fuck you.

I am not taking your bullshit anymore. You will be forgotten seconds after your funeral. I am one of the lucky ones who will be remembered for eternity.

Fuck you again.

I don't speak to you all at gatherings anymore because you all just criticize everyone else as well as me. You all act like you're perfect. This makes me feel at odds with myself. I will cut you all off from myself to be myself once again. Once again, I will be myself regardless what you all think.

"Like We Care."

I talked with 2 young teenage girls for awhile at my reading/book signing. The conversation was about "popular" music that is negative. One girl plays classical piano. Already things look good.

Will I collapse under the pressure, or rise above it all like a phoenix?

It is a figure of speech. It is a point of interest. Cleaning up your vomit after you savages have drank too much alcohol. Fuck you. You think that it is not fair to wait 45 minutes for your pop refill while I clean up another savage's vomit, savage? Even after you came in twice and made lewd comments to the women in the store? Fuck you. Next time YOU get vomit detail, savage.

"Tired Brothers"

The people who call me sometimes don't know english very well. I should get paid extra for being a translator.

He tells people shit that he should keep to himself. When everyone hears his shit they smile uncomfortably and nod. Frankly I don't care what medication he or anyone else is on. Plus, if anyone cares what medication I am on then you are being much too nosy.

It is raining everywhere.

So far the ride is pleasant, with the people who don't normally get along getting along. I will catch me if I can.

Finding a lottery ticket stuck in the cement in the pouring rain.

Now some rednecKKK is giving the waitress here shit, saying in a loud voice, "I had breakfast already at 5AM! This is dinner for me!" Shut the fuck up, asshole. That whole mess balances out the Swedes on the other side of the room talking with their mouths full. Shut the fuck up, assholes.

They say if we never forgot anything that we would go insane. I am not going to forget you and I know I am not going to go insane either.

Some young black kid talked to me yesterday while we were riding the bus. He said that he "flowed" as good as Jay-Z and that he was going to blow up this town.

You stink of cigarette smoke, stale beer and bad news.

I used to love your perfume, now it upsets my stomach.

They are all just dead weight. These are not good times. They are dead times, sad times, drought, war, famine disease and pestilence times.

There will probably be just a big party when they go. Hopefully not a bomb blast. They deserve a party and they deserve to retire early.

Am I out of line?

He glared at me with his eye that wasn't covered by an eye patch. Are you gettin' lippy with me, boy?

Famous last words.

How come a black man can have a shaved head and he is "cool"? And when I shave my head I am a Nazi? It is a hair style, not a lifestyle.

Sitting in the lunchroom on my break and listening to a young gangsta wannabe yak on his cell-phone about "bidnez."

Some asshole at the front of the bus with a guitar in a bag on his back is not letting anyone get on or off easily.

He just got off. Maybe I should too and go and kick his ass because of his ignorance of not letting seniors on very easily. What a jerk off asswad.

I used to take the same bus as this short guy who looked like a Filipino or something. He would always come up to me and put 2 fingers to his lips motioning for a cigarette. I would always say no.

This guy would get on the bus and sprawl next to women who spoke the same language as him. He would talk loudly and act like a real big shot. Did I mention he was really short? He definitely had short man syndrome.

One day the bus had to take a detour to the south side and Whyte avenue. The "midget" (as he will be known from now on) gets up and asked the bus driver, "we going to south side?" The bus driver said, "Yes, we are taking a detour." The midget asked again, "We going to south side?" The bus driver responds, "Yes, we are taking a detour." This went on another three times before the bus driver finally yelled, "YES, WE ARE GOING TO THE SOUTH SIDE!!! NOW PLEASE SIT DOWN!!!"

Everyone stared at the midget as he returned to his seat.

Infamous last words.

It is Father's day and I have got to work. At least my Dad liked his card I got for him. He has to work at this time too. I will be thinking about him.

You tell me that you have quit coffee and you have replaced it with fruit drinks that help with your memory. Yet you still smoke dope every day and you are an alcoholic. What is wrong with this picture?

Unfamous last words.

I had a long talk with my Judo instructor. He is 72 and looks good. His left knee is acting up so he has a hard time golfing. it is kind of a shame because he loves golf.

He had just gotten back from Japan and raved about the accuracy of the trains. Then he complained about how little space and how much pollution there is. It was nice to see him again. Sometimes I miss him. He is like a second father to me. I have known him since the fall of 1983, when I first started taking Judo.

Along with Grandma H., he is one of the most kind and patient people I have ever known. He should get a plaque with his name on it where I grew up. He helped out a lot of kids, including me.

I saw some big muscular guy with a shaved head and on his left forearm was a skull with a Nazi "SS" logo behind it. He was the same guy who when asked for some spare change from a homeless man responded, "No, but I have a spare piece of shit in my asshole you can have."

I get mistaken for morons like this all of the time. Look closer at me and you will see where he had a Nazi "SS", I have Curious George.

Again, it is a hair style, not a lifestyle. Although I am not condoning his ignorance. Non-famous last words.

I talked with 2 young struggling artists. Nice young guys. One guy was doing really cool things with paint and photographs of eyes.

One woman buys one and the artist asks her if he can take a picture of her and put it on his Facebook page. The woman says no because Facebook ruins lives. I totally agree with her after my mostly negative experience with Facebook.

She left me. I guess when you gotta go, you gotta go.

I saw 2 different shirts on 2 different muscle bound moron jocks....

The first: "Making love, something my girlfriend does while I am fucking her."

You sir are an asshole. I noticed that you were coming out of a tattoo shop. I bet you were getting a quote for some barbed wire around one of your biceps. Or better yet, something "tribal." Or even better, a Celtic design. Real original, asshead.

The second: "If you aren't a cowboy then you aren't worth a shit."

Boy that was a zinger. Actually I was thinking that if you ARE a cowboy, then you are a piece of shit. Left yourself open for that one fuckwad.

You get 2 assholes like this who probably have girlfriends that they don't appreciate. Then there is me. I have a hard time just making conversation with a girl I find attractive.

Those 2 guys are big fucking assholes.

Hope and anticipation.

I saw a guy I know last night. In the last couple of years, his Father, one of his brothers, and more recently, his mother have all passed away. He was really drunk. I guess he was trying to drown his sorrows. I just hope that his sorrows don't learn how to swim.

One tired brother.

My Grandfather B. was just diagnosed with cancer of the esophagus. He will meet a specialist today and have radiation later on.

Even though we sometimes disagree, I still wish him well. I know he will come through. He is one tough old bird. Good luck

Grandpa. I know that you will out live Grandma B. Not that Grandma B. isn't strong. It just seems you are stronger and/or lead a cleaner life.

Good luck Grandpa, good luck.

Is there anything more cliche than a black gangsta wannabe man flirting with and/or going out with a white, blonde haired woman? It happened 3 times last night and every time I go to this one nightclub it is the same thing. This time it was a pretty black boy flirting with the 2 white blonde haired bartender women. The blondes acted all coy and smiled at the pretty black boy. He even tried the same routine with a brunette until she shut him down by giving him the cold shoulder. It was awesome!

Now I am not saying that a black man can't or shouldn't go out with a white blonde haired woman. I just wonder if the black man thinks (even subconsciously) that he is spitting in the face of white men everywhere? Or if the blond woman wants to see for herself (even subconsciously) if a black man is that much more well endowed than a white man?

I sense over-compensating for an insecure position in life for the black man and blonde woman.

But what do I know?

Tonight was a blast!!!

Within a half an hour of being at work some guy in his early 20s, without a shirt on, falls in the middle of the doorway. I go over and grab him by his pants and I start to drag him out. He rolls over and is frothing at the mouth and he takes a few swings at me. I swat him in the chest and ask him, "Police or me?" He says Police. I start walking towards the counter and then I go behind the counter and dial 911. He begins spitting on my co-worker and I. I hang up the phone and tell him that the police are coming, so he leaves. The police are here within minutes and arrest him and give me a paper to fill out what happened. The officer asks me if I want to press charges. I say yes and he takes the jackass away.

Then I write in the store's communications book about the incident, adding that I had been threatened 4 times in the last 3 shifts.

An hour or so goes by and an ugly woman with no teeth comes in demanding change for the phone. I tell her that we are not a bank. She yells, "I am going to get you fired! I am going to come back here with a machine gun!!!"

I tell her to come back the next day at ten in the morning with her machine gun to get me fired, because that is when the store manager is in.

I get the communications book again and scratch out the "4" and replace it with a "5." Will I collapse under the pressure, or rise above it all like a phoenix?

It is a figure of speech. It is a point of interest. Cleaning up your vomit after you savages have drank too much alcohol. Fuck you. You think that it is not fair to wait 45 minutes for your pop refill while I clean up another savage's vomit, savage? Even after you came in twice and made lewd comments to the women in the store? Fuck you. Next time YOU get vomit detail, savage.

When will you crack?

Things are changing and no one can stop them. Your bigotry and lack of motivation will be your undoing. What goes around comes around. I will keep my head down for awhile and then come up for air. You will never get out alive. I will get out, hopefully intact while watching it all melt around you. 3 more weeks.

It will only last 3 more weeks and then the trip.

"I Am Just Plain Tired"

I get that hopeless feeling when a customer yells at me for no reason or when they blatantly lie. This guy is responsible for the phones and they never work. "Hello! Hello! I will try another phone! Just hang on a moment!"

I had dreams about sex last night. They were NOT about love.

One of my first calls at the call centre and the guy is doing bong hits. He croaks, "Here...." and then there is a bubbling sound.

This guy calls and he is very drunk. At this time we have a certain promotion on, he yells at me, "Corey, can I have the suck hole deal?!" I transfer him to customer service because at this time I was not aware of any promotion called, "The Suck Hole Deal."

The people who call me sometimes don't know english very well. I should get paid extra for being a translator. They say if we never forgot anything that we would go insane. I guess I can remember you and still not go insane.

A deaf woman turned me off of pornography, because porno owes my eyes something more than the constant bruising. There are people talking about other people being hurt emotionally and/or rejected like it was no big deal.

Now I am outside in the rain and all I can think about is my ailing Grandma Hamilton and how her dying is tearing everyone in our family apart. Needless to say, I have forgotten about my money woes.

They are all just dead weight. These are not good times. They are dead times, sad times, drought, war, famine disease and pestilence times.

It is raining everywhere.

Even though I am not a religious or spiritual person, something in me hopes that Grandma H. and Grandpa H. are with each other now. I can only hope.

I will catch me if I can.

I haven't seen you in 6 years. You are just as beautiful as I remembered, if only I was in a better mood.

I am now sitting alone in a single motel room in Manitoba waiting for my Grandma H.'s funeral tomorrow. You are gorgeous.

I wish that I could talk to you but I am in a lousy mood. I will go to bed alone, again, alone again.

How come a black man can have a shaved head and he is "cool?" And when I shave my head I am a Nazi? It is a hair style not a lifestyle, shithead.

Sitting and waiting for my first meal of the day. I am a long way from home yet when I am here I sometimes feel closer to this place than home. So much history is buried out here. This is where I would like it to end. I am at peace here, whenever I am here.

I am now sitting alone in my single motel room worrying about my Dad and thinking about my Grandma H. who just passed away. With her passing a whole generation of my name disappeared.

My Dad is now the oldest of my name.

Without Grandma H., it is now history the past, the past history....

I was a pall bearer along with my 2 younger male cousins, my youngest sister's husband, Wayne (who took care of the Hamilton farm) and Mickey, who was a pall bearer at my Grandpa H.'s funeral too. He was the town practical joker but both times he was a pall bearer for my family he looked serious and tired. Maybe because we both felt it was an honor to be a pall bearer for my family. Mickey twice, myself once

You stink of cigarette smoke, stale beer and bad news.

If their order is late by even one minute, then they call back yelling. Is this the biggest problem in your life? If it is, you must have a pretty easy life.

Are you gettin' lippy with me, boy?

There are these 2 women in wheelchairs at the call centre. One of them used to always ask me to go and pick her up so she could get in from her vehicle in the parking lot. Every time she had me wheel her in I, along with her, was always late. Finally I said I would not go get her anymore. Now, finally, she always comes on time. Stupid cow.

The other woman is always spreading rumors, like, the call centre is being closed, we are all going to get laid off and such. In addition to this, she is always complaining about everything from her job to her life in general. Just another stupid cow.

I used to love your perfume, now it upsets my stomach. Am I out of line?

A woman at work, who seems to have more mental health issues than me, asks me what I was writing. At first I was going to say, "None of your business." But I was a nice guy and said, "Just some ideas for poetry." I wish people would mind their own business.

She left me. I guess when you gotta go, you gotta go.

The cute Asian girl I smiled at returned the smile but still would not sit next to me.

He gave me shit this morning.

Even though this bums me out, it can't burn out the fact that I just saw a woman that I haven't seen in almost 20 years. She was so excited about a possible new career. It was cool to see her so happy. Maybe I will see her again.

The last three days have been cloudy and raining, sometimes with thunder. When will it end? Maybe in August when I pay off my student loan? Maybe not until winter? I get so moody when it is like this. It makes my walks longer than they really are. Oh well, I could be dead from a tornado, hurricane or earthquake.

I am waiting in the hallway for the call centre to open. The guy sitting around the corner from me is about 3 inches taller than me and about 120 pounds heavier. He looks 360 pounds or so. He is 30 years old and still lives in his Mother's basement. He is critical of everyone else. The next time he does criticize someone I will go face to face with him and ask him if he has ever kissed a girl.

Once when I went into the washroom he was popping a pimple on his face. While I was taking a leak he was making strange sounds. I walk around the corner and he is making farting sounds with his hands under the running water. He may very well think that I am a dink. This is fine with me, especially when it is coming from someone who talks to himself out loud. I just think he is pathetic because he is always acting like he knows everything. I think that he must be over compensating for a pathetic life.

I thought about it afterwards and wondered why I did it to begin with. Now I feel like vanishing into the air and hoping no one will find me. I often wonder if everyone feels that way at some point in their life. Maybe I will never know the answer to these questions.

I saw a sign for catholic schools the other day and it said, "faith and choice." I can see the faith part, but choice? Do they give out free birth control or offer pro-choice views or do they offer courses on Atheism? Probably not. "Choice." What a fucking joke.

I had to take the train today because it was quicker than taking the bus. I was running late for my appointment at my doctor's office. The stairs I had to walk up from the train reeked of urine.

I HATE taking the train.

I saw a poster that said, "Art without critics is nothing." BULLSHIT.

Art without critics is everything and critics without art are nothing. There is no school for being a critic. There are just people who like art and people who don't like art. There are just people who can NOT do art and people who CAN do art. Critics are the for- mer. Critics are what I wipe my ass with.

You don't meet our standards.

You are using up a bunch of the company's benefits plan.

The one before that, one of the bosses would swear at me and call me names. Eventually they went bankrupt. Like I always say, what goes around comes around.

We do not want you around anymore.

The one before that I made an off colour joke that got me fired.

I have a list as long as my arm about how I did not meet any of my employer's standards. The moral of the story: be different, like wearing a "FCUK" shirt, but not mental illness different.

Now I have found a job that pays OK, is easy and the bosses and most of the other people there that I work with are nice. This is the happiest I have been in years.

It is Father's day and I have got to work. At least my Dad liked his card I got for him. He has to work at this time too. I will be thinking about him.

I have another migraine at work again. These migraines are getting to me.

At my high school graduating ceremonies I was happy to get out of there until some guy yelled, "Get off the stage ya fuckin' skinhead!" Moments later a friend told me to smile. I was nearly sick to my stomach.

I was going to meet a friend downtown and I decided to cut through the mall and go to the washroom down stairs. The escalator was not working and an elderly, mentally challenged man was walking down very slowly. Not that it mattered because I had time to spare.

A young lady in a suit and dress came up right behind me and sighed loudly. As the three of us were getting off of the escalator she said to the mentally challenged man in a loud, angry voice, "Next time take the elevator!"

She was tired but just another bitch too, because she might as well have asked him to explain the theory of relativity. Next time I see you, bitch, I'm going to punch you in the face and then hug the mentally challenged man.

Is there something I should know about you? Is there something I should not know about you?

I was listening to The Police's album, "Ghost In The Machine" today. During the first 30 seconds of the first song, "Spirits In The Material World," the power in my apartment building went out. It did not come back on for a little more than an hour.

Last night I was sick. Sick in the stomach, head and heart. I dreamt of needing condoms. I dreamt of a writer so controversial that rock stars copied him. I dreamt of hiding in the shower of a train infested with spiders. It was so hot and everyone was mad all of the time. Then the train went into freezing cold weather unexpectedly. I dreamt of working at a grocery store. Then I woke up and told my nastiest secrets to someone on the internet, hoping that they wouldn't be pissed at me or alienated by my actions. Last night I was sick. It carried over into the morning and I am having a rough time right now. No one seems to notice, the right now. I should go now, right now.

They told me to write all of this stuff down. You know the stuff, me hiding in a snow bank in elementary school to avoid bullies. I am leaving a popular haunt of mine to get cash because their debit card machine is not working. Then I was hiding from the rain in a used bookstore. I bought a bunch of Bukowski, then getting the cash nearby and going back to the ol' haunt to pay and then going home.

On the way home I saw the 2 young, pretty girls who were worried about getting beaten up on the Ave. Then buying a couple of lottery tickets, then going home and stripping down to my underwear and turning on the fan. Laying in bed just in my underwear listening to R.L Burnside and reading the Bukowski that I just bought. I am in trouble again and I brought it on myself and now I am waiting for a miracle. It will happen. And when it does they will all tell me to write it down again, and then my work will be done.

I continually make mistakes and my family continually rubs it in my face. I continually do what I want to do and my family considers what I want to do mistakes and they continually rub it in my face too.

Months ago I told them that I no longer wanted to go to family gatherings because of them all rubbing it in my face. This is my first non-mistake in awhile and it feels great and right and now I am the happiest I have been in years.

I have been reading a lot of Bukowski lately. Some of it early on in his life and some of it later on in his life. I really believe that when he had cancer and was on his deathbed, he could relate to the tired sisters of the world. Early on in his life it seemed like he made women into tired sisters.

I can relate to some of his work but most of it I think of as being great art.

I was on the bus last night and someone punched me lightly in my left shoulder. At first I ignored it, then a young girl's voice asked, "Did that hurt?" I turn around and the young girl with blonde hair and big boobs was referring to the tattoo on the back of my head. She was wearing just a pink tank top and pink short shorts. I told her that all tattoos hurt. She responded by saying, "No they don't." I was going to tell her that I have 35 tattoos and then ask her how many she had but there was no point. She appeared to have no tattoos, I wondered if she was even legal to drink. But there is no point in arguing because she was just another pretty dumb ass.

On my way to the nearest 7-11 to get my slurpee fix, I saw a beautiful young woman with a very young boy. She looked to be in her mid 20s and the boy looked to be 4 or 5 years old. I recognized her, but I just couldn't place her face. I went into the 7-11 and as I was getting my slurpee, she was right behind me with her little friend. I finally placed her, I took the same bus as her in the morning and she used to work at a coffee shop near my place.

I introduced myself and she introduced herself and the little boy. I introduced myself to him and now I knew their names. Maybe I will see her (them) again and we can ride and chat on the otherwise lonely bus.

Two grubby girls say in unison, "Nice tatties!" I say thanks and walk to work thinking about the nice Chinese girl at work. She is very pretty and has a calming yet upbeat demeanor. I would like to get to know her. Maybe, maybe.

I am intimidated by their beauty.

The Chinese girl I work with and the beautiful blonde girl with the 5 year old son that I just met. The blonde's son is good looking just like her. Too bad she smokes, or at least I think that she does. I just wish that I could get past the smoking thing with a woman.

The cute Chinese girl that I work with is only 20 years old. Today she was supposed to sit next to me, according to the seating plan, but she had a supervisor move her to a completely different area of the call centre.

Yeah, I feel good now. I just want to go home and sleep right now.

The numbers don't add up, or at least they don't seem to. Story of my life. I can hardly wait until I get the number "13" tattooed on me. If "13" really is bad luck, then so be it. I have never had a bad Friday the 13th.

1) because it is Friday and the weekend is up next.
2) because sometimes it is a payday.
3) because the numbers almost always add up.

She is a nice, mature young girl and she is always happy to see me. Too bad I am 20 years older than her.

Hope and anticipation.

Shattered the other day. Almost everyone here is fake or an ugly version of reality. The flaky hippy woman who lives above me said that she wants to meet with me when she gets back from her trip. She said she wants, "to have time to honor a new friendship." What the fuck is that supposed to mean?

I haven't seen her in awhile. I took the same bus we used to take at 4 different times over the last month and she wasn't on any of them. I hope that she isn't avoiding me and that she is just on holidays with her son or her work schedule was changed around. I hope that I see her again.

You are why I don't get romantically involved with with women...er...I mean girls 5 years or younger than me. Fucking brats.

The other night at a movie I ran into you. You were all smiles and young with your wedding band. I assumed your other half was the guy who scowled at me. I have often wondered what it would be like to kiss your beautiful mouth.

On my way to work I ran into you. I wish I had not run into you. You said the same thing to me today as you did last time. You will call me, we'll meet up, blah blah fucking blah. I wish that you would be honest and come right out and say that you did not want to see me or talk to me again.

Fucking asshole.

I hear your voice whenever I work at my first job. Your voice makes me want to know you better. It is very gentle. I know that I will never get to know you because I am old enough to be your father. You are a beautiful young lady.

All of the pretty girls at work, or at least the 4 that I like, seem to just talk to me to give me a bone. They seem like they just tolerate me. Some day I hope to evaporate and do my work and listen to music and read books.

I'm allowed to dream, aren't I?

Last night a man with a cute blonde haired 3 and half year old girl came into the store. The girl was very happy so I stuck a $1.99 price tag on her. She and her Father leave. Moments later they come back in with the mother as well this time and asked to see me. The three of talked a bit and all of a sudden the little girl asked, "What's wrong? You're making triangles!" Apparently I had myhands on my hips and when she sees someone doing that she thinks that they are angry or upset. Cute little girl.

Cute little family.

The cute Chinese girl at work quit. I guess it is a waste of time getting upset that she never told me that she was quitting. Just another flake sister.

She is not going to invite me to her 18th birthday. I guess it makes sense, I am twice as old as her and her friends. I would probably be a drag or worse yet embarrass myself and her. It is probably for the best.

I picture myself kissing a pretty girl on the lips. She is a smoker. I picture myself having sex with her and while I am sucking on her breasts, second hand smoke is transferred from her breasts into my mouth and down into my lungs.

I will never again kiss a woman on the lips if she is a smoker.

I see your young slender body at work and I wonder what it would be like to lay in my bed with you. And then I see that other guy chatting you up. You now pay more attention to him than me. Sometimes it will be just you and I talking and he will barge in.

After all of this happening in one day, I bow out and go home all sad and lay in my lonely bed, lonely and alone.

My youngest sister and her husband are having a baby. Her, my other younger sister, my mother and my father all think that I would make a lousy father because of my illness. My half-brother is the only one who is supportive about me some day becoming a father. His support is greatly appreciated. My family's lack of support is typical and not appreciated. I am tired.

Tired. Tired. Tired.

Tired of everything not working out. Tired of always struggling. Tired of always going up hill. The Chinese girl, the one who just quit at work, thought it was strange that I was not close to my family. I felt like telling her my life story and then seeing what she thought. Not that it matters what a 20 year old brat thinks.

I am tired.

I know that I will make a good uncle. I know that I will make a good father. I just need some rest because I am tired. Tired.

Tired.

Tired.

I cannot forgive you for letting me down. You were supposed to be there for me when everyone was letting me down. I know that I should forgive you because we all make mistakes, but forgiving is not in my nature.

Believing in what goes around comes around is in my nature....and sometimes I am sorry for this. I tell no one when I am sorry, though. No one of importance anyways. If I brought in on by myself then that is a different story, but you letting me down was not brought on by me. Thanks for opening my eyes. I am not sorry.

I am going to take everything in my own hands. After this you will be first in line to apologize to me.

SLURPEE EMERGENCY!!!

I just got home from the 7-11. I was moving around 40 pound "bibs" of slurpee syrup. There was no way the 2 ladies working there could do it, There was just no way. Their legs and backs would not have held out. The other workers won't do it, even though they could.

Tonight.

First - a very drunk man stumbles into the store swearing at the other customers and such. He is about to put a sandwich in his jacket when I ask, "Can I help you?"

He stumbles over with a seven dollar sandwich and throws down four dollars in change. I tell him that I cannot sell him the sandwich. He asks if it is because he is native. I respond, "No. One, you are drunk. Two, you are rude. And three, you don't have enough money. Now go before I call the police." He swears at me and says that he is going to get me at the end of my shift.

Second - a drunk homeless man who has been barred from the store comes in. I remember him from 2 weeks earlier when I let him in. I tell him to leave and he holds out his hands imploringly. Again, I tell him to leave or I will call the police. He tells me that he is going to straighten out my head as he leaves.

Third - a young woman comes in and buys food from me and compliments me on my good service, then she leaves.

About 15 minutes later she comes back in to buy junk food and water. I tell her what is on sale and both of us get confused. I ask if we can start over. I then introduce myself and she introduces herself. Between the both of us, we figure out what I need to get for her. I find the water in the cooler and again she compliments me and leaves.

Fourth and final - a young woman comes in and buys some cigarillos, asks for ten dollars cash back and asks if I can call her a cab. I ring up the sale, give her her cash back and call a cab for her. She thanks me for my good service and says that I am a lot nicer than that "battle axe" that was in earlier. I console and thank her and she leaves.

I finish my shift and she is outside smoking and waiting for her cab. She thanks me again for the good service. What a strange juxtaposition and/or dichotomy of an evening.

I just finished my shift at the 7-11 and I am talking with a co-worker outside in the cool morning air when all of a sudden you come hurtling towards us on your pink bicycle. Nearly crashing into your handle bars and smashing up your pretty face.

We talk a bit and suddenly I have the urge to hold you. You are the same girl who bought water and junk food off of me a few nights ago.

From what I see and hear from you, I get the feeling you have quite a story to tell.

It is all coming to a head, a climax if you will. I told someone off today because one of her friends is a bitch to me whenever I come into your store by myself. When I come in with two certain friends and/or the owner is in she is always nice to me.

The bitch is the fake tired sister I spoke of earlier. You know the one. She won't listen to reggae because it is too black and yet she will listen to hip hop? Hate to break it to you, babe but all music, except for bagpipes and classical was created by black people. You had better get your history straight, darling.

From now on, when someone shits on me, I will call them on it, for it is all climaxing or coming to a head if you will.

I am in one of my favorite haunts and my hands are sticky with jelly. My nose is sticky from all of the good smells and my ears are sticky from good music and gentle talk. All of which I currently do not mind. When everything ends, I will come here to decompress.

All of the elderly who can't make up their fucking minds will be gone soon enough. Unfortunately a fresh batch will be here in no time to replace them.

Shit.

I hope that I do not end up like them.

Moments before the last drop.

I am contemplating the process. The process of seeing you, talking to you, hearing you, listening to you, touching you and being with you. A light blinks off on off on off on above my head while I write this down. I am not even sure that you will show up here today. I try to relax, watching the nicely dressed people contrasted with the saturday casual shopping people. There will be more later on when I am closer to the last drop.

Overall it was a good day for once.

I did not see any of the girls that I wanted to see, but I met some cool people and a bunch of friends showed up. Sincere thanks to all of the people who came down and made my day great!

Fuck you all who ruin my days. I am not going to take it from you anymore. It will all work out, whether you all ruiners support me, or not.

Whether or not you support me, I will march on. I decide this in one of my regular haunts. This time it is loud and busy, which suits me fine at this point in my life.

Will I collapse under the pressure, or rise above it all like a phoenix?

I am in one of my haunts. The owner and I each have a shooter of tequila to celebrate the day. I haven't drank alcohol since my birthday in 1999 and even then it was just a shooter. Something sweet, if I remember correctly. My last serious bout of drinking was in 1998, I had 3 pints of beer. I was so screwed up afterwards.

Anyways, that was the past and this is to the present and the future. Cheers, Miss, cheers. And if I haven't said it before, thanks, Miss, thanks.

I could tell you about the jackass kid who worked at the call centre for 2 weeks and on his last day he acted like he was the best agent ever and that him leaving was special. Then I could tell you about the East Indian kid who put the word "cunt" on a lady's bill and got fired for it. Everyday after that, these 2 East Indian girls defended him. The four people I just spoke of are fucking idiots who should never be allowed to leave their respective homes again.

It is a point of interest. It is NOT a figure of speech. Cleaning up your vomit after you savages have drank too much alcohol. Fuck you. You think that it is not fair to wait 45 minutes for your pop refill while I clean up another savages vomit, savage? Even after you came in twice and made lewd comments to the women in the store? Fuck you. Next time, YOU get vomit detail, savage.

When will you crack?

Things are changing and no one can stop them. Your bigotry and lack of motivation will be your undoing. What goes around comes around. I will keep my head down for awhile and then come up for air. You will never get out alive. I will get out, hopefully intact while watching it all melt around you. 2 more weeks.

It will last only 2 more weeks and then the trip.

"Re-Introduce Yourself Because It Is Finally Complete"

Do I scare you?
Do I scare you all? Sometimes?
Most times?
All of the time?
All of the above? Some of the above?
Or none of the above? Sometimes I scare myself.

Although you may be afraid, I am never afraid of the ending, at the ending. It is something that should be celebrated! Do you hope that I am living with the living? Or do you hope that I am dead with the living? Or do you hope I am dead with the dead? Or do you hope that I am living with the dead?

I am not afraid of the ending anymore.

I don't think that I ever was afraid of the ending. Have a nice day, month year, life.

I am out of here...

...for now.

Hopefully I will see you all soon again.

No thanks again.

All thanks again.

See you soon.

Started this piece in
May, 2008 in the town of Rossburn, Manitoba.
Finished this piece in
September, 2008 in the city of Edmonton, Alberta.

Lonely Night Poems
&
Lonely Night Photographs

Character

I am bleeding
From all of the little lies
So I shower myself
In little words and myths
So that I won't give in
Make faces at me
And act friendly
So you don't have to
Grow up
Your chair is comfortable
Mine never is
That is what pushes me
To get better at my craft
And to be a better person
Change
You don't
I do
You won't
I will
With or without you
I will grow
And stop all of the bleeding
And showering
Until I tell myself
That I believe in my self
With or without you
And the way I feel
It will be without you

#1602

Houston, We Have A Moron.

I beg your pardon
But I did not ask for
Your opinion
I beg to pardon
You
But you do not deserve
My respect
Because
Respect is like love
Respect is earned
Not given away freely
Just because of age
Or disabilities
If you are a rude
Asshole
Then no matter your condition
I will dish it
Right back
Pardon you?
No
You are not worthy
Of a pardon
Or of love
Or of respect
From me

The Son Who Wasn't

I had to do it
The 8 or 9 years
Of it was killing me
Killing me inside
Making me feel all sad
And alone
Every day
Every night
I thought that I was a bad son
Then I thought that
I was the good son
And then I realized
I wasn't either
I was a human
With feelings
That kept on getting hurt
I was a human
Who had had enough

We parted ways
Not letting each other
Know how much pain
We felt
Deep down inside
I felt that
I knew that
It was time
And that it had to be done
Broken hearts
And bruised egos
Are not needed
On a regular basis
And I had to
Put a stop to it
Put some distance
Between us
So I could breathe
Once again

#1604

Anger Is Not The Lottery

I think of my Grandmother Hamilton
Who is falling into dementia's grasp
And how she kicked a nurse
Who was being bossy
I am upset
At how angry my
Grandmother got And I think
That is not my Grandma
I knew when I was 14
The Grandma who would
Make me gingerbread men
So I let it go

Tonight I am walking home
Down the avenue of fools
After a pleasant evening of poetry
The weather is gorgeous
I am waiting for the light
To change
On the corner of the Strathcona Hotel
The green turning light goes amber
And then the walk light blinks on
I am crossing the street
And suddenly and almost simultaneously
I hear, "Look out!"
I see a car speeding towards me
It hits me and I use
Its momentum to roll onto
The hood
And then back onto the road

And suddenly and almost simultaneously
I see red and yell obscenities
I am going to kick the shit
Out of the male driver
But he drives away
One of four boys between 18 and 23

Shouts, "Hey man, he's pulling over!"
The driver gets out of the car
And the boys start egging me on
"Kick his ass, man!
We'll back you up!"
I walk briskly over
To the driver
Yelling at him
And with the intention
Of putting him in traction
I realize
That the driver
Is talking slowly
His speech is slurred
And he is wobbling towards me

I then think of my Grandma
Kicking the nurse
Then I think that this driver
Is not worth it
If I beat him up
I am basically condoning
My Grandma's tantrum
By having one myself
I tell him to be more careful
And I go get a slurpee
As I am walking home
I realize
That I have an old lottery ticket
In my wallet
And I think to myself
Wouldn't it be funny
To win the lottery
On the night
I am nearly killed?
I get home
And turn on my old computer
And I go online to check the numbers Nope
Not one number was a match
And then I think
Wouldn't it be even funnier
To win the lottery
On the night that

I AM killed?
Er....
I guess not
Knowing my luck
That is exactly what would
Have happened
If I had died
A million bucks in my pocket
And then I think
It could get worse
And then I think that
There is another lottery tomorrow
And another sunrise in the morning
That hopefully
My Grandma and I
Both get to see
Because it can only get better
I am alive
And it can only get better

7UP And Wrestling

He closed his eyes
And put his feet up
On the coffee table Drinking directly
From a 2 litre bottle of 7UP

We watched "Stampede Wrestling"
On a warm summer afternoon
In Manitoba
"Let's watch some wrastlin', Corey!"
So we watched
The semi-violent soap opera
I knew that the next morning
We would go for a walk
On his land
Not saying much
To each other
Just enjoying each other's company
And watching the Ravens and Magpies
Coast on the early morning breeze
6AM and it was the sunrise
That woke us up
Grandma slept in
But by the time we got home
Breakfast would be started

Now he is gone
The house on his land is gone
The land is owned
By the five kids
Because Grandma
Is falling into dementia
Now she is a star
That I will see
For the last time in a few weeks
And then the next time
Will be her funeral
I tried calling her 3 times
On her birthday last week

And she hung up on me
All 3 times
She just has not figured out the phone
I just hope that she remembers me
When I see her

Grandpa did remember me
And then months later
He was gone
I told my Dad that
This would be
The last time I see her
My Dad said solemnly
That that was fine
So in a matter of weeks
I will be with
My slipping Grandma
Hoping that
I say all of the right things
And that she remembers
Them for a little while
I just hope that she doesn't suffer
Like her husband
My Dad's Dad
My Grandpa

I closed my eyes
For the day
And I dreamt
Of all of our younger days
When no one suffered

The Place Just Ain't The Same

One hour
Before she says
So many things
But it is just a dream
Anyways
Because the place
Just ain't the same
Since her days
Summer is coming
And I want to be
On my best behavior
An apology may never come
But if it does
I want to be
On my best behavior
Driving on the highway
Where dreams stopped
Coming true years ago
Green green grass
Cool cool breeze
Over the farm
I don't understand
This need to be
Out there
When it was crushed
Years ago
I am tired
I am so tired
Of just being your toy
For your pets
To chew on
Then discard
After a year or so
Words are lost
On your ears
Apologies never come
From your mouth
To my ears

Because
You are always right
And
I am always wrong
In your eyes at least
You hold grudges
For our past
I hold grudges
For our present
I never raised my voice
Until you were both born
And then my voice
Was lost in all of the commotion
Of another World War
I think to myself
If I leave now
Would you all notice?
Probably not
Because you are all
So busy with
Your cars
And your pets
And your houses
And your jobs
To notice
When you have
Fucked me over
Again
And again
(This time for real)
I boycott your events
Until you realize
That you should be
Held accountable
For your actions
And words
Directed at me
Hey look!
I have a credit rating!
And you know what?
I am going
To shove it in your face
Until you finally

Respect me
For who I am
Not for what I look like
Or how heavy
I have become
Earlier today
I bought a lottery ticket
Out of desperation
Knowing full well
That even if
I won the big one
You still would not
See me
You say that you worry about me
And in the next breath
You criticize my lifestyle
Guess what?
I don't like your lifestyle
Much either
So reluctantly I tell you to
Fuck off
Until you get your shit together
And until I feel
You will finally take responsibility
For your actions
Happy birthday
Merry Christmas
Happy New Year
Happy Easter
Happy Mother's Day
Happy Father's Day
Not until you stop
Your judgmental bullshit
And release me from
Your grasp
And I escape from
Your grasp

Hawks And Geese

When my Grandma
Saw me and my Father
Her face lit up
Like a child's
On Christmas morning
She said that I looked different
My beard had thrown her off
She had lost a lot of weight
And her eyes were glazed over
Nevertheless
She was happy to see us

There was snow all of the way there
And thousands of Geese
At least 3 different kinds
And they were waiting to go north
We saw as well dozens of Hawks
My Dad and I stopped
At a small restaurant
In Saskatchewan
Then went straight
To Grandma in Manitoba
The towns had gotten smaller
And I think that my Grandmother
Has run out of gas
She is pretty much wheelchair bound
And if she walks
It is with a walker
And only about 20 feet
We had lunch with her
And she kept asking my Dad
To get her her purse and some cheques
My Dad said he would
Even though he won't
Because one of my Dad's younger brothers
Is the only one with
Signing authority
And the farm is owned

By my Grandma's five kids
My Father being the oldest
We watched cartoons
But Grandma couldn't keep up
And she told us that
There was an unfinished quilt
In the basement of the farm house
She said that myMother could have it all
The farm house was torn down 6 years ago
But at least she is happy
That my Mother is quilting
One day my Dad and I
Went over and she looked tired
And some of the nurses
Told us that she was being difficult
And kicking and hitting
Some of the nurses
And she was eating very little if at all
This was hard to take
Because my Grandmother
Doesn't care anymore
She seems to have
Run out of gas
And no longer wants to live
It won't be the last time
I talk to her
But it will be the last time
I see her
I want to remember her
On one of her better days
My Dad and I say
Our goodbyes
And we leave
The melting snow
The Geese, the Hawks And the small dying towns
For now
I took some photographs
And they will be there
For me when
She slips away totally

I am happy that I got to see her
Even though at first I was apprehensive

Because of how much
My Father had said that she had slipped
I am sad
That it was the last time
I will see her
I am happy
That she was happy to see me
I am happy that
I told her that I loved her
Something that I forgot to do
To her husband, my Grandpa
Before he died in 1990
But that is for another poem
I miss you already, Grandma
And by the way
Thanks for everything, Grandma
There is a head on my shoulders
And it is full of conflicting emotions
This head knows how tough it is
But also knows how much
Fun I had with her
And how much
I cared for her
And she like wise
There is a head on her shoulders
And it was saddened
At the memorial
Of over 2 dozen men and women
Who died over the last year
In the home where she lives
If your God is with you Grandma
Make sure that he doesn't make you suffer, please

Thanks again for everything, Grandma
I love you very much
And this one is for you
And all of the small dying towns
And all of the snow and Geese and Hawks
You will never see again
I truly hope that your God
Is gentle with you Grandma
Love,
Your Grandson, Corey

No Artificial Colours

I begin this story
A little differently
I have been called
Many things
And years ago it hurt
Sometimes very badly
But now it doesn't warrant
Even a drop of ink
Unless
Unless I have caused
Someone else hurt
Indirectly or directly
Today someone broke
My trust in them
And it involved innocents
Which may have broken
Their trust in me Sometimes
Very rarely
But sometimes
I feel like quitting
This whole procedure
And starting over
Somewhere else
And this time
Being more careful
So much more careful
The new innocents may say
I am artificial
Sometimes
Most often
Sometimes
I have no artificial colours
But when it causes
Someone else pain
I sometimes
Feel as if I should
Censor myself
And not show

My true colours
And not show
My heart on my sleeve
So as to not cause
Anyone pain
I know regret
Is regrettable
But I can't help it
But to regret
Causing
Others pain
That I hope this little
Apology eases your pain
And that it is a learning experience
For me

For Good

Let's be honest
I just can't taste it
Anymore
Actually
I never could
I just kept on
Piling it on
Until you backed away
For good
I try not to be negative
But the last few days
Have been tough
And I have taken it out
On you first
And me second
This has been
One of the few times
That I have been horrified
By my own actions
I was in too deep
In something
I have never felt before
So I opened my eyes
And took another shot
And all of the time that
Went by
I could have saved up
And retired on
Let's be honest
When something bothers you
And no one else
Then it is all
In your own head
And it is time
To move on
And start again
Let's be honest
As long as I learned

Something from it
Something from nothing
Then it was
All
Worth it

#1610

Thank You, Come Again

I did not mean
What I just said
Because
I have not seen my hometown
In years
And I hope
That someday
I can go there again
Just this time
With you

Last night
I had a dream
And you
And your friends
All gathered around
Trying to wake me
Because you all thought that
I was tossing and turning
Because
I was in the midst
Of a nightmare
And when I woke up
I was saddened
Once again
The first time
I was saddened
Because
I fell in love with you
And then I overwhelmed you
With my intensity
So you left
This time
I was saddened
Because
In my dream
You did not leave
And we lived

Happily
Ever
After

Fading Regretful Memory

The night is a long trip
Just like crossing the Atlantic
By boat
And a fading memory
Is all that remains
Of you and your smile
The regret I have
Is as hard as the concrete
That you walk on
To your job every day
The snow whistles
Around my head
Thanks to a strong wind
And the realization
That I pissed you off
Rattles around inside my head
Just like the loose change
In someone's deep pockets
All of this stretches out
The long snowy overcast day
Like it is getting ready
For a second round of winter
When it felt like
The first round was over
Shit
Just give me a crack
Of light
So I can believe
That summer is coming soon
And give me another crack
At being near you
And I promise
I promise that
I won't ruin your weekend off
So you can actually relax for once
And not go into work on monday
Pissed off
Pissed off at me

For breaking your back
And as for me
I will do my best
Not to be like 4 billion
But to be like one in 4 billion
Who would like to
Get to know you
I promise that
I will do right by you
And I promise that
You won't be disappointed
By me ever again

I look outside my window
Then back at this
Lonely piece of paper with some ink on it
And I can't help but to feel that
In a way
This is my obituary
For any promise
There may have been
In me getting to know you

Young, Arrogant And Vacant

You ask me
Why everyone in this city
Is so arrogant
Jokingly I tell you that I don't know
Because usually
I am allergic to people
Then you give me a bunch of shit
I will pay you to shut up
I will pay you to leave me alone
I will pay you to go die
I will pay you to answer
Since when is killing
Your central nervous system
With drugs and alcohol cool?
I will pay you to answer
Why most people 25 years or younger
Have no work ethic
And feel everything
Should be handed to them
Like spoonfeeding a baby
Arrogance is in your blood too
So a rage as hard and as sharp as nails
Boils up in me
To beat you silly
Dar Williams said
"Teenagers kick our butts"
What?
Are you that fucking stupid
To believe that shit?
Teenagers and young adults
Only kick butt
If they are drunk and/or high
And if they are looked at
One too many times
Fuck you, Dar Fuck you, too
Because I am not happy
In my current state
Always apologizing

For who I am
For being
Romantic, neurotic, passionate,
Schizophrenic, creative and angry
Fuck you all
Fuck all young people
Who have dreadlocks and piercings
And who do drugs and alcohol
FUCK YOU ALL.

Watching the game At a local bar
Knowing that and
Realizing that
If I had the money
I would buy my way
Into a stupor
To forget
That pill popping teenager
Who alienated me and
Brought me down
I could have been your's
But your parents
Were absent landlords
And mine were
There for me most of the time
To kick my ass
When I strayed
And to push me
To do better
I could take that alcohol
NOW.
And instead
I go to sleep
Worried about
Some young piece of shit
Not worth worrying about
This all fades out
As I try to sleep it off
Because it is over
And maybe I should
Just let it go
And hope that no one else
Lifts my rock off of me again

Since when is it a problem being gay?
Maybe it is a problem
In your narrow mind
But it is most likely
NOT a problem with someone
Who is actually gay
You are a very small person

#1614

Last Message To Infinity

Let me tell you this
For the last time
My work is for me
And was for me
And my own cathartic
And sometimes therapeutic reasons
I don't do this
I didn't do this
For your entertainment
This note
Is most definitely
NOT for you
If you like it
If you liked it
Bonus
If you don't like it
If you didn't like it
Tough
I do this all
I did this all
To get better at it all
In my eyes
That is what drives me
That is what drove me
I was never here for you
I was never there for you
After I am gone
The same rules apply
Because I will never fail
With my work
Because it is was for me
And when I pass on
To the forgotten infinity
Burn me down to ashes
And if I don't have enough money
To cover an urn
Then you can use a fucking coffee can
For all I care

Then take it to that cemetery
In Rossburn, Manitoba
Where my Grandparents,
My Great-Grandparents and
My Great-Great-Grandparents are all buried
And toss the fucker
As hard and as far as you can
Over the edge of the cemetery
Into the valley below
To the west of that cemetery
And if you can get
A spot there for me
Put on a small stone or plaque...

                              Corey Wayne Hamilton
                                    Born - Died

                            And as for the epitaph?
                            That is an easy one...

                                "Take It Or Leave."

Young Elitist

"I liked their first album best."
Don't fail to start the day
By continuing to be a young elitist
"Their music is too angular."
What the fuck does that mean?
Are you now getting
Geometric on my ass?
The chick with the
Cuban dictator hat said
"There are no hits
On the new album."
And if commercial radio
Ever caught on to them
And they did have a hit
All of you yahoos would be the first
To cry, "sell out!"
Or say again
How much you liked
Their first album
I have heard this bullshit
From young fuckheads
About bands like
Weakerthans, Interpol,
Constantines and The Hives
And the fact of the matter
Is their song-writing and music
Are far more better
And far more eclectic
Now, than it ever was
You just tow the party line
Because you are a young elitist
Who thinks it is cool
To be there when it all started
When it doesn't matter one bit
Because you won't stick around to the end
The world is on fire
And all you want to do is bitch about
A band changing?

Possibly for the better?
Are you really that
Naive?
Petty?
Stupid?
I guess you are
Because elitism is
A young person's disease
And the cure is
Not having anymore children
And
Killing off all the ones
Who are 29 years and younger

Working On Sundays

Last Sunday
At the bus stop
Sat an Aboriginal man smoking
And swearing
Because the bus wasn't there
He started talking to me
But I really did not want to
Talk to anyone before work
1) Because I had a migraine
And 2) Because, generally speaking, I don't like people
Besides my friends of course
He complained that
Once when he was drunk
He got caught jay-walking 3 times
And now he could not get I.D.
Because he had $1500 in fines
I guess I was supposed
To have sympathy for him
But
1) I don't drink alcohol
And 2) I don't jay-walk
So I had no sympathy
For this simpleton
The bus comes
So I let him on first
So I can sit by myself
Last week it was a christian
Now this
What's next?

Maybe I should just quit
Working Sundays?

#1617

At Home

What happened
In your car last night
With him?
Where was my weather
When I needed it?
I could have been serious
But I bungled that one
And I had to move on
Again
He was the hero
And I was just
A casual onlooker to you
As the two of you walked away
With a newspaper
Over your heads
To cover yourself
From my weather
I just can't muster enough up
For a light show
So I go in the opposite direction
And sleep it off
At home
With the windows open slightly
Until
Until
My home is no longer
A bad weather prison
And until
Until
You can see past your car
And him

Since Then

Leave some daylight for me
I was everything you wanted
Then I spoke my mind
And we had a falling out
And that is when
It started raining
And it hasn't let up
Since the last time
I saw you
And you saw me
Is this how
It has to end?
This is what
I forgot to ask you
When I had the chance
And now it is far too late
And it has not stopped raining
Since then

I guess at least
When I go out
You can't tell if I am crying
Or not
Until the rain ends
And I know
I just know
It just has to end
Soon
Because nothing lasts forever

#1619

Leave My Rock Alone

To all religions
And religious people
Including muslims
And christians
And the like
Leave me the fuck alone!
I am an Atheist
And I don't want your views Pushed down my throat
I keep my Atheism to myself For the most part
But when some religious person Lifts my rock off of me
It makes my blood boil
I did not ask for this
But you insist
On forcing it on me
I will admit that
I do have a soft spot
For Buddhists
But that is because
They don't force
Their beliefs on you
The rest of you do

Now remember this
Before you send me
Your religious rants
I did not ask for them
I do not want them
So
Once and for all
Leave me and my rock alone

Haunts Me

Making a pretty, deaf woman
Do pornography
And making her say "whore"
And taking advantage
Of someone with a disability
Is just not cool
Degrading someone
Because they don't have something
That you have
Is horrible
And I hope that it comes back
To haunt you
The way it haunts me
I feel like
Taking the lives of the men
And helping the pretty, deaf woman
Get dressed
And walk away from losers like that
I truly believe
What goes around
Comes around
And that these men
All get crippled
And then the pretty, deaf woman
Can turn the tables
And laugh at them

#1621

I Would

I would
If I could
See you in the flesh
Wish it all away
The urge
To touch you still
Comes to me at night
Like the cool, night time, summer breeze
Through my partially opened window
Then when my pockets are full
The emptiness
Goes away briefly
I know
I know
I know
You are taken by your god
And I am taken by myself
And the trains shall never meet
But
I would like us to meet
Quietly
If we could
And see if we could
Mix the pot some
And move together as one
Just like the cool, night time, summer breeze
Through my partially closed window
I would
If you would
And I could
If you could

You Had Better Run

Elementary school I was constantly
Made fun of
And beaten up
I remember once
My glasses got broken
During a fight
And my parents
Called the parents
Of the kid who did it
And they told my parents
That I was lying
My parents believed them

Once before school had started
In the winter
I was being made fun of
While another kid
Said he was going
To beat me up at lunch break
So during morning recess
I dug a hole
In a nearby snow bank
And I hid in it at lunch
He never found me
And after school
I ran home

In junior high
The beatings slowed down
But the verbal abuse
Did not
It was so bad
I had to get a locker
Away from everyone else But then I discovered
Judo
And people
Started to give me space
And high school was still hell

But I got by

Then
Last week
I met you again
The first time
In nearly 20 years
You were still
Tall and lean
And intelligent
And pretty
The last time I saw you
You showed concern for me
Because I was all whacked out
On mushrooms
You always showed me
A great deal of respect
And your respect
Got me through
Some tough times
I am not sure
If I returned the favor
But if we meet again
I will make sure that
You know
You have my respect
Even after all of these years

Canada Day 2008

Heavy duty
Light duty
Fuck off
Fuck on
What do you know
About me?
Waiting around
Feeling guilty
About not being
Able
To make rent
Because it is my own fault

But then I see you
And your beautiful girlfriend
And your young child
And I wonder why
You stopped calling me
I just wanted to ask,
How am I supposed to learn
From my mistakes
If friends don't tell me
When I have fucked up?
With people like you
I guess I will never know

Then I see you
At the pub
And doing well for yourself
I remember New Year's eve, 1990
When a former friend of mine
Was seeing you
And he went out
With a different girl that night
Canada Day 2008
You and I were both drunk
And someone prevented us
From thrashing outside
From the party inside

I felt bad for you Anyways
That former friend of mine
Used to make fun of me
For still being a virgin
Anyways
I am glad
You got past his ignorance
And made something of yourself

Day after yesterday
Rent day is coming closer
And I can't make it
And it is my own fault
And I hope for
Some sort of "divine intervention"
That can cure me
Once and for all
I am dead to the world
If it stays the same
I will have to slip away
After I bolt the door

Fuck on
Fuck off
Light duty
Heavy duty
No matter what it is
I start feeling down
And thinking that
This is all my fault
I have to realize that
Some of it
Is my fault
But most of it
Is not my fault
It is just
How the cards
Are dealt
So
Lighten up Already!

#1624

This Is How

I lost the drugs and alcohol
Waiting for you
Then I gained a bunch of weight
When I realized that
You were not coming back
All over the world
This happens to all sorts of people
Lose one step
And then you are off track
For good
This is my room
It is where everything starts
But where will it end?
When will it end?
How will it end?
And
Who will end it?
If anyone
It should be me
Or circumstances
Beyond my control
Yes
This is a bad time
Because
I am no one that you know
And because
I am like the frightened rabbit
This is how
It will stay
I am no one that you know

#1625

Under My Door

Slide a note
Under my door
I have been listening
To you
Living above me
For months now
And I have been waiting
For a note
Under my door
For all of my life

For part of my life
I sat close to her
Then
All of a sudden
She asked to be moved
And hasn't talked
To me
Since
What can a lonely boy
Like me do?

Slide a note
Of hope
Under my door I really need it
Now
After all of this denial
And rejection
Slide a note
Under my door
One that makes me
Not have a lonely future

#1626

Patti Smith's Lament

Everything is holy
When the day
Lasts an eternity
Loss of a husband
Loss of friends
Loss of peers
Loss of inspiration
Because of all the pressure
Because of all the days
Because of all the dead authors
Because of all the loss
Just tell them
You have had enough
And go live on a farm
Somewhere close to nowhere
With your children
With your medals of honor
With your medals of honesty
With nature
Go
Go now
You have earned it
You need a rest
At least I believe you have earned it
At least I believe it to be
Maybe after you rest
The days
Won't be an eternity
And you can
Come out again
To tear it up
Once more
Just like the holy days

#1627

The Rye In The Catcher

He is still lost
Looking for salvation
And we are nearly
At the end
Of our path
I just don't get it
Being a copy cat
Your salvation
Is a rip off
Why go that way
When you end up
Not able
To find your way
It is 2:14 in the afternoon
And there is
A bunch of noise
Outside
And I am on
The inside
Hoping that you are alright
And that he
Will find the right path
Not a copy cat
Not a phony
But of a Roman Candle
Or one stick of dynamite
The three of us
Are having the
Nearly lost blues
He is having
The phony blues
She is having
The nearly hit blues
And I am having
Both of those blues
As well as
The worrying blues about
The phony blues

Being nice to people
Who don't care about me
The nearly hit blues
The am I going to make rent
This month? Blues
And the worrying blues
All of the above

I hope that the three of us
Can find our way soon
For no one
Can live these blues
Forever.

#1628

Despair Is A Vitamin

Thinking about you
And taking you out
For your 18th birthday
Not to get you drunk
Not to get in your clothes
Along with your body

When I turned 18
I was with a friend
Who worked at the local pub
We shot the shit
And he let me try
All of the beers
It was a small pub
Run by an Asian man
It was all special to me
Or at least that part
Of the evening was
I never got to tell you
How special that time was
Then our friends
(As good as their intentions were)
Took to me to see a band
Called "God"
I remember buying a shirt
After that I don't remember
Anything else
I blacked out
And woke up with
A hangover in my bed
I should have said "No"
To our friends
But I was scared
That I would offend them
I would like to take you out
Buy you dinner
And a drink
And just talk

Just like I did
In the early part of my 18th birthday

I would hope that
You are honest with me
And that if
You don't want to
You would not be
Scared to tell me
For I would not be
Offended if you said "No"
In fact
I would respect you all the more

#1629

Would I See You There?

Finished reading
A nightmare book
And it made me wonder
If I would ever see
Grandma and Grandpa Hamilton
Again
My atheist brain says, "No"
But my idealist heart
Hopes that I will see you both
Again
Days like this
Make me sad
To be alive
When so many I know
When so many I knew
Are not here
With me
Parts of me
Are not here
With me
Too
They went away
With the family and friends
Who went away
For good
I have my own problems
I wish to escape from
And see you all again

Maybe
I should just sleep it off?

#1630

Again And Again

When you open up
They all want
To wander in
And make a mess
And then they take what they want
And leave you
As empty as a husk

Last night I dreamt
Of old friends
I had not seen in years
A sharp pang hit me
In my stomach
The sharp pang
Was how much
I missed them all
I would do
Anything in the world
To see them again
But maybe it is
Not in the cards
Uh oh
There's that sharp pang again
Telling me
That I should not
Open up like this
Because

When you open up
They all want
To wander in
And make a mess
And they take what they want
And leave you
As empty as a husk

Turning that sharp pang
Of missing someone

To a sharp pang
Of never opening up
Like that again
And never leaving my home
Again

#1632

The Year That Passed Away

I hear the noises
Of happy school children
Waft in through my open window
Along with the cool fall breeze
There is an elementary school
Near the apartment building that I live in
And I hear all of the happy children
On their lunch breaks and recesses
Stay happy little ones

My Dad's Mom passed away
This past May
My Mom's Mom passed away
This past Sunday
Both passings tore holes
Through the family
Big enough to drive a bus
Through
My Dad's Dad passed away
18 years ago
That was the first time
I had seen my Dad cry
The second time
Was at his Mom's passing
Now my Mom's Dad
Has been diagnosed with
Cancer of the esophagus
I ask my Mom
If there is any hope
She gets all choked up
And replies
That the doctors
Will make him comfortable
But that he will be on a liquid diet
For the rest of his life
I just hope that he can make it
To the New Year
Or at least Christmas

I call Grandpa
And my Aunt answers letting me know
That he figured that
He needed a new fridge
So he bought a new fridge
I ask to talk to him
When he says, "Hi"
I tell him that I wish
I could take it all away
And that I am at a loss
For words
He says
That there is nothing
Anyone can say
I tell him that I love him
And he says thanks
And that when he saw Grandma
In the funeral home
That she looked so beautiful
That he thought
She was going to get up
And leave with him
When I hear this
My heart rips in two
And I say that she was a beauty
Grandpa sounds tired
So I let him go to bed
Hopefully with peace

I hear the noises
Of happy school children
Waft in through my open window
Along with the cool fall breeze
I have always liked the fall best
Because change came along
With a cool breeze
I now wonder if there is
Too much change this year
It seems to me anyways
That people are very resilient
We flex with the change
Or crumble under the weight

I think of all of the children
Outside my window
And I hope that any change
That occurs to them is gradual
So that they can flex
Their little heads and big hearts
Enough to handle the pain
That sometimes shows its face
It seems that the younger we are
The more we can take
This upcoming November
Would have been my Mom's parents'
65th wedding anniversary
The noises of the children
Help me drift off into sleep
In the middle of the day
With the thought that
It will get better
With every passing day
It is just the "now"
We all have to get through

I think about the noises
Of the happy school children
Long after they have left school
For the day
And I think about
How it has been a tough year
But something inside tells me that
It will get better
With every passing day

Johnny Bower Lost A Fan

This is kind of mixed up
But hopefully it will make some sense
My Mom's Dad
My Grandpa
Served in two wars
The Navy in World War 2 and
The Army in Korea
He always had stories to tell
I only remember one being sad
In World War 2 he served
On the H.M.C.S. Sackville
The last Corvette in the Canadian Navy
He told me this story
Of a friend of his
Serving on the same boat as him
Who was responsible
For firing bombs called "hedge hogs"
Into the water
Whenever they exploded
It meant two things
The first
Was that a German U-Boat was hit
And that the U-Boat was now sinking
To the bottom of the ocean
The second
Was that my Grandpa's friend
Would start vomiting into the water
Because he thought that that was
The worst way to die
Sitting at the bottom of the ocean
Waiting for the oxygen to run out
Overall Grandpa rarely talked about the wars
I didn't press him either
My Mom told me once
Grandpa punched a Captain in the nose
And lost his stripes over it
That sounded about right
Grandpa was pretty stubborn

Sometime after the wars
Grandpa met Leaf great Johnny Bower
Grandpa was a big Leafs fan
And to meet a star
Was a highlight to him
Grandpa had a supportive wife
And they were like two peas in a pod
Grandpa and Grandma had
Two lovely daughters and
Several Grandchildren and
Great Grandchildren

In his later years
Grandpa made these quirky birdhouses
For the family
He quit smoking when I was born
And years later he quit drinking
In August of 2008 doctors found
A cancerous tumour in Grandpa's throat
Then on September 14, 2008
Grandma passed away
And Grandpa's stories stopped
At least it seemed that way to me
These last two events seemed to take the wind
Right out of Grandpa's sails
I saw him in the hospital a few times
Getting radiation treatment and such
The stories had ended and
Most of the time he slept
On Friday April 10, 2009
Grandpa suffered a stroke
And four days later
On the evening of April 14, 2009
Fred Arthur Barnard passed away
Just two weeks shy
Of his 88th birthday
It is times like these that
I ignore my atheist side
And right now
I would like to think
That maybe
Just maybe somewhere
Grandma is having a drink and

Listening to Grandpa tell his stories
And although they miss us
And we miss them
Grandma and Grandpa
Are having a great old time.

"Lonely Night Songs"
Is dedicated with love to:
Grandma & Grandpa Barnard.
Irene Ellen Barnard August 2, 1924 to September 14, 2008.
Fred Arthur Barnard April 29, 1921 to April 14, 2009.

Thanks.

www.ingramcontent.com/pod-product-compliance
Lightning Source LLC
Chambersburg PA
CBHW081352080526
44588CB00016B/2463